Saving Animal Babies

Amy Shields

NATIONAL GEOGRAPHIC

Washington, D.C.

Thanks to all the people who love and care for animals, especially Mary Fleming, Dr. Greg Mertz, Dr. Lori Perkins, Justine Brewer, and Dr. Laurie Gage. —A. S.

The publisher and author gratefully acknowledge the expert assistance of Ron Tilson of the Minnesota Zoo Foundation.

Design by YAY! Design

Paperback ISBN: 978-1-4263-1040-9
Library ISBN: 978-1-4263-1041-6

Photo Credits

Cover, Ron Kimball/www.kimballstock.com; 1, DLILLC/Corbis; 2, Peleg Elkalay/Shutterstock; 4-5, Erik Beiersmann/dpa/Corbis; 7 (UP), Horst Ossinger/AFP/Getty Image; 7 (LO), Imaginechina/Corbis; 8, Smithsonian's National Zoo; 9, Smithsonian's National Zoo; 11, Andrew Cunningham, Cummings School of Veterinary Medicine, Tufts University; 12, Andrew Cunningham, Cummings School of Veterinary Medicine, Tufts University; 13, Southwick's Zoo and Belinda Mazur; 15, Courtesy of Zoo Atlanta; 16, Courtesy of Zoo Atlanta; 17, Courtesy of Zoo Atlanta; 18 (UPLE), Vanderlei Almeida/AFP/GettyImages; 18 (UPRT), Suzi Eszterhas/Minden Pictures; 18 (LO), Martina Stevens, Houston Zoo; 19 (UP), John MacDougall/AFP/Getty Images; 19 (CTR), Yu Qibo/Xinhua Press/Corbis; 19 (LO), Steven Good/Shutterstock; 20, Alex Mustard/2020VISION/naturepl.com; 22, © National Aquarium; 23, © National Aquarium; 24, Dr. Greg Mertz; 25 (UP), Dr. Greg Mertz; 25 (LO), Dr. Greg Mertz; 26, Dr. Greg Mertz; 27 (UP), Dr. Greg Mertz; 27 (LORT), Dr. Greg Mertz; 27 (LOLE), Dr. Greg Mertz; 28 (UPRT), Sarah2/Shutterstock; 28 (UPLE), photomaster/Shutterstock; 28 (LO), v.s. anandhakrishna/Shutterstock; 29 (UPLE), Vitali Burlakou/Shutterstock; 29 (UPRT), Dimj/Shutterstock; 29 (LE CTR), Diane Macdonald/Getty Images; 29 (RT CTR), Picsfive/Shutterstock; 29 (LO), Marina Jay/Shutterstock; 30 (UP), Imaginechina/Corbis; 30 (LOLE), Ferry Indrawang/Shutterstock; 30 (LORT), Simon Greig/Shutterstock; 31 (UPLE), Derek R. Audette/Shutterstock; 31 (UPRT), Dougal Waters/Getty Images; 31 (LOLE), Ekkachai/Shutterstock; 31 (LORT), Mint Images RM/Getty Images; 32 (UPLE), Franco Tempesta; 32 (UPRT), Courtesy of Zoo Atlanta; 32 (LE CTR), Zurijeta/Shutterstock; 32 (RT CTR), Erik Beiersmann/dpa/Corbis; 32 (LOLE), Shutterstock; 32 (LORT), © National Aquarium; header, Potapov Alexander/Shutterstock; vocabulary boxes, Vule/Shutterstock, nemlaza/Shutterstock.

Printed in the United States of America

13/WOR/1

Table of Contents

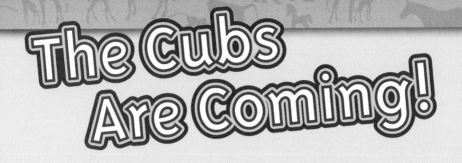

The Cubs Are Coming!

It is a dark and quiet night at the zoo. The tiger is restless. The zookeeper thinks the tiger will have her babies soon. And she does.

Tiger babies are called cubs.

There are four new tigers in the world! Tigers are in danger of becoming extinct. That means every tiger is special.

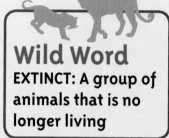

Wild Word

EXTINCT: A group of animals that is no longer living

Eat, Sleep, Repeat!

This is the tiger's first litter of cubs. Some tigers don't take care of their first litter. Without help, the cubs could die. But caretakers at the zoo know what to do.

At first, the cubs only need to eat and sleep. Every three hours, the cubs drink warm milk.

The cubs have a blanket that smells like their mother. Sleep well, little tigers.

Wild Word
LITTER: All the babies born to an animal at one time

Would you like to try a chunky meat milk shake? The cubs are crazy for them.

First the veterinarian checks the cubs' baby teeth. They need to be strong and sharp to chew the chunks. Then the zoo chef buys jars of turkey baby food. He mixes it with milk and vitamins to make the milk shake.

The vet sees that this cub's teeth are healthy.

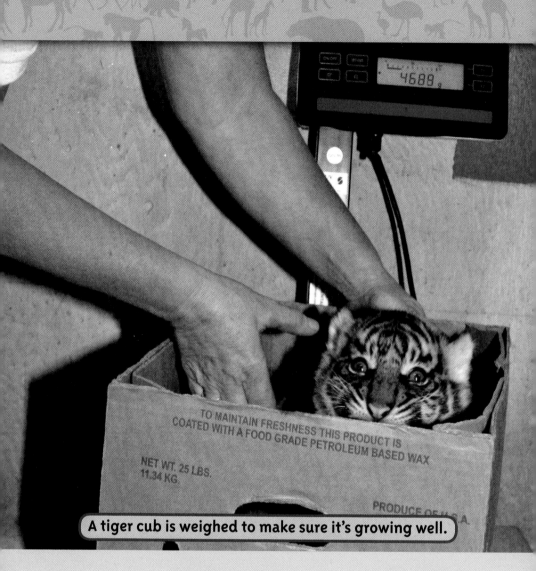

A tiger cub is weighed to make sure it's growing well.

Now the cubs will grow even faster. One day they will be full-grown tigers.

Wild Word
VETERINARIAN: A doctor for animals, called vet for short

A Long, Tall Baby

Molly is three days old. She is an 80-pound, 5-foot-tall baby giraffe. This baby should drink three gallons of milk a day. But her mother cannot make milk for her.

Molly also has an infection. She needs help. She has to go to the hospital.

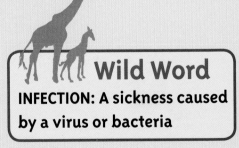

Wild Word

INFECTION: A sickness caused by a virus or bacteria

The vet feeds Molly milk. The tube in Molly's neck is held in place by a bandage.

The vet puts goat's milk in a giant baby bottle. She has to hold the bottle up high for Molly.

The vet puts a little tube in Molly's neck. It doesn't hurt and is an easy way to give Molly the medicine she needs.

Soon Molly is better and back with her mom.

Molly is healthy and growing. She is almost as tall as her mother!

Wanted: One Hairy Mom

Remy's mother got sick before he was born. She could not take care of Remy.

Orangutans need to be raised by other orangutans. Remy needed a foster mother to take care of him.

Madu is a grown-up orangutan. She never had a baby of her own.

But she had cared for two other orangutan babies that didn't have moms. Would Madu be a foster mother to Remy, too?

Wild Word

FOSTER MOTHER: An animal that is not family but cares for a young animal like a mom

Remy is an orangutan baby. Young orangutans stay with their moms for five to seven years.

Remy snuggles with Madu.

With his blanket and toys, Remy went to meet Madu. It was love at first sight. Soon Remy climbed on Madu's back.

Remy watched Madu. Madu taught Remy what to eat. She showed him how to hang and climb. Remy learned how to be an orangutan.

Madu teaches Remy how to hang with one arm.

17

Toys for Tots

All babies love toys. Zookeepers try to get the right toy for each baby.

Sloth babies cling to their moms. A stuffed pillow works, too.

Even the youngest monkeys can learn to hang from ropes or chains.

Elephants love splashing and swimming in water. A kiddie pool is lots of fun!

Polar bear cubs like to chase and pounce on a ball.

A treat frozen in ice is a puzzle for curious panda cubs.

Young tigers like to play with each other. Another tiger is better than any toy.

Saving a Seal Pup

Guinness is a gray seal, just like this one.

Even ocean babies need help sometimes.

Wildlife rescuers saw a seal pup on the beach. Seals leave the water to rest. But this little guy was too thin. He didn't go back in the water. He was in trouble.

Rescuers wrapped him in a wet towel and took him to the hospital. They named him Guinness.

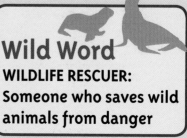

Wild Word
WILDLIFE RESCUER: Someone who saves wild animals from danger

Guinness had a broken jaw. The vets operated and put a wire in his jaw. The wire held the jaw together while the bone healed.

Three months later, Guinness could eat by himself again!

Guinness enjoys a frozen fish in ice—called a fishsicle.

It was time to go back to the water. Everyone cheered when Guinness scooted back to the ocean where he belonged.

Backyard Babies

Do you want to be a vet when you grow up?

You might want to be like Dr. Greg Mertz. People know him as the Odd Pet Vet. He takes care of all kinds of animals that need help.

Dr. Mertz helps a snake.

This three-month-old goose has a broken wing. The bandage works like a cast on a broken arm.

This painted turtle has a cracked shell. The bandage keeps away infection.

People bring hurt animals to Dr. Mertz. Many wild animals get hurt on roads. Luckily, Dr. Mertz can help most of the animals he sees.

Springtime is busy for Dr. Mertz. That's when many babies are born. Animal babies like to explore. Sometimes they get into trouble and need help.

Dr. Mertz to the rescue!

These opossum babies were found in the wall of a house.

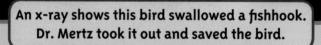

An x-ray shows this bird swallowed a fishhook.
Dr. Mertz took it out and saved the bird.

Raccoon cubs can live on their
own after three months. Until then,
Dr. Mertz keeps this one safe.

A baby starling needs
to eat every half hour
around the clock!

Dos and Don'ts

What can you do to help baby animals? Here are some dos and don'ts . . .

 DO slide a ramp in a pool if you see baby frogs in it. Then they can climb out safely.

 **DON'T** feed ducks and other birds bread. It's bad for them.

 DO wait 24 hours before rescuing a baby deer or bunny. The mother is probably nearby.

DO

tell an adult to call animal rescue if you see anyone hurting an animal.

DON'T

adopt a wild animal. They do not make good pets.

DO

prevent pets from harming wildlife. Put a bell on your cat's collar. Keep your dog on a leash.

DO

pick up trash you see in the woods. Plastic bags and bottles can hurt animals.

DON'T

pick up a baby bird that is on the ground. Ask an adult or call a vet or the local Audubon Society for advice.

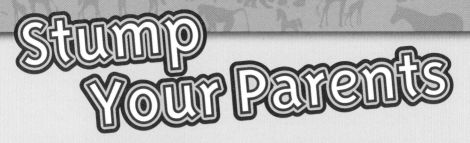

Stump Your Parents

Can your parents answer these questions about baby animals? You might know more than they do!

Answers are at the bottom of page 31.

1

When tigers are born, they
Drink Milk .

A. Drink milk
B. Are hungry for meat
C. Don't sleep
D. Sing

2

What do young orangutans learn from older orangutans?

A. How to find food
B. How to hang and climb
C. How to be an orangutan
D. All of the above

3

What should you do if you find a baby bird on the ground?

A. Run away
B. Leave it alone and tell an adult
C. Bring it home
D. Give it some candy

4

Wait 24 hours before rescuing a baby deer or bunny because _____.

A. It likes to be alone
B. It might be out getting a snack
C. The mother is probably nearby
D. It could be on its way to a party

Where does a seal pup live?

A. In the mountains
B. In the ocean
C. In the forest
D. In a department store

5

6

What do elephants love?

A. Chocolate
B. Reading
C. Water
D. Doing jumping jacks

What kind of milk can you feed a baby giraffe?

A. Chocolate milk
B. Goat's milk
C. Soy milk
D. Milk shakes

7

EXTINCT: A group of animals that is no longer living

FOSTER MOTHER: An animal that is not family but cares for a young animal like a mom

INFECTION: A sickness caused by a virus or bacteria

LITTER: All the babies born to an animal at one time

VETERINARIAN: A doctor for animals, called vet for short

WILDLIFE RESCUER: Someone who saves wild animals from danger